Beautifully Broken
Poems about Depression, Anxiety, and a Family Broken Apart
Emma Eiler

Chaos Hatter Publishing

Copyright © 2024 by Emma Eiler

All rights reserved.

No portion of this book may be reproduced in any form without written permission from the publisher or author, except as permitted by U.S. copyright law.

This book is dedicated to all the people that have struggled through mental illness or still struggling through it you are not alone and you are never alone. Also for those people that have felt alone or unseen.

You are seen and not alone but most of all you are loved.

Most importantly keep fighting your life will get better.

Contents

A Letter To You Dear Reader	1
1. Being a Puppet	3
2. The Dusty Path	5
3. My Life	7
4. Pain	10
5. Not Perfect	12
6. Mirror	15
7. The Real Me	17
8. Time	19
9. My World	21
10. Reflection	24
11. The Keyhole	26
12. This Place	28
13. Fake Faces	31
14. Someone Else	33
15. Trust You	36
16. World of Ruins	38
17. No Superhero	40

18.	The Movie	43
19.	How could you?	45
20.	The Clock	47
21.	Alone	48
22.	A Few Seconds	50
23.	An Evil History	52
24.	Tell Me How I Should Be	53
25.	Begin to Fade	54
26.	Listen!	56
27.	I'm Your Hero	58
28.	Should I Cross the Road	60
29.	Because of the Fighting	61
30.	The Real War	62
31.	The Warm Sun	63
32.	The Special Wind	64
33.	I'm Sorry	65
34.	The Show	67
35.	I am The Wind	69
36.	No One Will Come	72
37.	Written on the Wall	74
38.	I Don't Belong	76
39.	I am No Better	78
40.	Simple Words	79
41.	Nothing Just Nothing	81

42.	Just Go!	82
43.	People Always Leave	83
44.	The Words of Life	85
45.	Freedom	87
46.	No One	89
47.	The Coming of Dark Times	91
48.	The Place I Used to Call Home	93
49.	At the Bus Stop	95
50.	Locked Away	97
51.	Escaping Reality	99

A Letter To You Dear Reader

Dear Readers

First and foremost I want to say thank you for buying this book of poetry. All the poems that have been put in this book are very near and dear to me. I wrote these poems not only to get my feelings out but to also show that no body in this world is alone and your feelings that you feel are valid. I have been diagnosed with depression, anxiety, and ADHD. I was officially diagnosed when I was an adult and I went numerous years feeling like I was abnormal and that I was broken from how other people were. I have found through the years that there is nothing wrong with my broken pieces and that everyone has broken pieces. But the thing that so many people do not realize is that you can go through all of that and see the good in people then like me, you are beautifully broken and the world needs more people like us in it.

Love you always,
Emma M Eiler

Being a Puppet

My shadow upon the wall
Begging to not be this way
But it's hard to let it go.
For to long she was the one
I could talk to
About my feelings
And not feel like a total fool.

She explains to me she is tired
Of being a puppet and
Hates following my every move.
She is dying to get away
And not be the same.
Little do I know how to free her
But I know I want to do the same.

No longer can I do this.
Play this stupid game
Against someone not human
Knowing I can't win.
I'll be playing this game forever
Never being able to leave

As I am stuck in this fake world.

For I am her
Only to be seen in the light
The broken parts of me
Never seen.
Because they are hidden
By the Darkness
Which fills me up inside.

I shout out
For someone to save me.
But they all just point and laugh
As if it were some grand show.
Soon the lights fade
And all goes black.
Making me lose myself
Forever.

The Dusty Path

The path is long and dusty
The footsteps are vanishing quick.
The time is passing you by
As you take your time.
You wonder where this path will end.
What will happen then.
Who you will be with at that time.

Others come along the path
Some stay for only a short while
While others stay longer.
It seems the more you travel this path
The less you really want everything.
You realize friends don't always stay
And family moves away

But yet we still walk down the path.
Sometimes we are cold and alone,
While other times we're happy and warm.
Sometimes you feel like you can't go on
And that you will stop right there.
Yet somethings pushes you on

And tells you to not give up.

So as you sit there
And decide what to do
I hope you realize you need to go on
And you can't fail.

Because the one you love
Is just ahead of you
You are following their footsteps
And their waiting for you to catch up.
So don't let them down.
Keep your eyes on whats in front
Reach your hand out to find them
And grasp it

My Life

Ones close together
The other ones far apart
Spread out along the road
Like a broken heart

Death do us part
That's how it is
Family is family
And that will never change

Death, lying, cheating
That is what a family is filled with
But we cant help it
That's just the way it is

Why does life have to be like that
Why can't we have joy.
Instead of all this pain
That consumes us in the darkness

Leaving no trace of the happiness
Ones felt

And the darkness always fills us up
And making us suffer this way

But that is just
What it is to be human
Since that Apple was eaten
We are doomed to be this way

I think of the Garden often
And that story of Adam and Eve
How it may have been a test
But it shows the errors of humans

Nobody is perfect
We all have cracks upon our souls
Put there by others
It doesn't matter how old.

Why is this the way of life
What did we do to deserve this
Why does our souls
want to learn this lesson

How can we be whole
by learning to be broken
But these questions
Should not be asked

We should just sit there and smile
Our way through the problems

Through the pain
For this is my life.

Pain

People don't understand
All the pain I've seen
And people think it
Doesn't effect me
But it does
And it kills
Anymore pain
I think I'll explode
I shouldn't be seeing
It all I'm only 14
And haven't got time
I learned all my lessons
Early in life
And people don't know
It kills
Every night I think
Of ending my life
But then I think of
All the pain it would
Bring to myself and others
So I don't do it
I know I have been told many times

That life will not always
Be like this
And to just give it time
But time is running out
And I sit here
Against this wall
And cry
For life is hard
And as hard as I try
Nothing
Takes
The
Pain
Away

Not Perfect

How would you
Like me to describe my life
It is perfect
Every aspect is perfect

Well it's not
Nothing is ever perfect
It is just a word
Misused and misunderstood

Because nothing is ever perfect
It is a lie that we tell ourselves
A standard that is impossible
To achieve

And for a person
As broken as me
It is something
I will never be able to get to

No matter how
High I climb

How far I run
It is just out of reach

That is when the
Depression
Sinks in the most
When I think about it

It would be impossible
To know
By looking at me
I look happy and carefree

You cant tell how a person feels
By their clothes
Their smile
How they walk and talk

The only thing you can tell by
Is their eyes
There is where the soul lies
That's where the secrets lie

And even though
I try to hide it there
It is impossible to do
Would you look

Even ones
To see the pain

I carry
For never being able to be

Perfect!

Mirror

I grip the knife tight
It's just nice knowing it's there

Close to me
Inside my hand

I would never use it on anyone
Not even myself

The thought has crossed my mind
And the pounding never stops

I look at myself in the mirror
Seeing an image that I hate

I take my fist to it
And look at the shattered pieces on the ground

I pick it up
And start to cry

Realizing what I did

I look into the broken pieces

I see my past
And then my future

I see who I will become
Knowing that they are not me

The one I hate
Looks back at me

And I see a devilish smile
On their face

But then it is all gone

Replaced
Just
Like
Me

When I look back
I am looking into

The black nothingness

The Real Me

You look at me
I look at you.
You turn your head so fast,
I know you don't look into my eyes.
A lot of people don't,
They are afraid that if they do
They will see hurt and pain.
But it is not my fault,
I cry every night.
The more I'm ignored,
The more pain I get
Everyday and night.
For you see
That is the thing
The world ignores me.
I am alone
In a room that
Is so full.
Screaming at the
Top of my lungs
And nobody reacts.
But people don't know

The real me,
I look
Act
Talk
Laugh
And do everything different.
But you don't see that,
I may not look
Or act normal.
But I am the same
As everyone else.
I just need
Someone to see me
And tell me
That everything will be okay.

Time

Look at the time
It flows by

With every step we take
But we need to realize

That life goes by
And we have no way of
Stopping it

Even if you wanted to
You can't
Rewind, fast forward, and stop

Even when you want to
But you can't
Life is weird like that

You can't do anything to stop it
Even when you try everything
But nothing works in the end

That is the sadness
That one holds

So hold those moments
Dear to you

And never let go of them
They will stay with you forever

Until slowly the memory fades
And we are all lost forever.

My World

This is the world
I created

This dust
And ashes
The lies
And the hatred

All burn here
Because of me
Because of my choices

The little demons
Dancing in my head
The sadness that consumes
My very soul

It hacks away
Leaving me empty inside
I am a shell of a person
Screaming to escape.

Calling out
To nobody
This world is empty
Just like me

But that is okay
Because why do we need others
When in every shadow
And whisper of the Wind

There is a friend
For don't you see
Those have been the ones
That were there for me

Wait
Why do you scream
Is my world not to your liking
Or is it me

Don't run inside this world
The demons will think it is a game
One that you will not win
Come back

As I see the demons run
Wild and fast
they catch you
And bring you back

BEAUTIFULLY BROKEN

Welcome to my world
Where no one ever leaves
The demons trap you
and make you stay

But this was not the world
I first built
The decay was caused
By the tears and the words

The words
Uttered from others lips
Brought the demons
out to play

So you see
It wasnt truly I
Who created this world
It was all of you.

Welcome to my world.

Reflection

I look at you
You look at me
You see the things you hate the most
And that can't be

As you turn to leave
You see me do the same
You lift your arm
Mine does the same

You walk up really close
And put your hand up to the wall
Mine follows suit
You don't feel it

But I feel your cold hand
It lays against the glass
The glass in which I am stuck behind
Forced to move like those
Who look into the mirror

I have hated those people

BEAUTIFULLY BROKEN

The ones who have always laughed
And never really cared
But then again nobody really cared

They would come up to the mirror
Like you did
And see if I would really follow
Like you did

And I would
So they would have there fun
And then they would leave
Leaving me

Why does no one care
For the one stuck behind the mirror
Asking how you are
But never do they care

This glass that I am behind
Is only cold because of them
It is the truth of their soul
But never will they know.

I went my whole life
With no one that really cared about me
Everyone is to worried about themselves
Until the day when someone cares
I will go on stuck behind this mirror

The Keyhole

An eye through a Keyhole
Peeking in on something that is hidden
It's behind a closed door
Away from the world
In a room with no windows
How could someone be that cruel

The eye is gone
Afraid of what it saw
Not wanting to see again
The ugly beast within
It grinds its teeth
And it looks at them with its evil eyes

I look through that keyhole
I see a little girl
Sweet as can be
I use that key that is around my neck
To let the thing out
The thing that you fear

The beast comes out

And lets that world feel her rage
The people run and hide
But I am by her side
People are afraid of the power
That she holds

But why should one be afraid
From the very monster that they made
The rage and fury that consumes
the monster
Was put there by them

The cold eyes
Look for the prey
The one that locked them away
With the words that
Were the binding chains
And the acts that were the cage

I have freed the beast inside of me
For we are one and the same
And now the people that
Have wronged me
All run away

Scared of the thing
That they created
And this beast will not rest
Until they all have paid.

This Place

Can I walk this world alone
Only seeing the people who died
They see me too
They grab for me

But they can't touch me
For I am doomed to be here
In this cold world
I find no warmth anywhere

How can I live in this place
I sit down
Just to pass the time
The river flows behind me

I touch the water
It does not make my hand wet
I don't feel the temperature
I can't feel anything

I am numb to everything
I can't feel your touch

BEAUTIFULLY BROKEN

You hover around me
But you don't get a response

You put your head down
And walk away
Because you don't get the feeling
From me that you want

For it is not only you
But everyone that has come
They all try but dont get a response
And soon they leave

But that is the thing
I know that they will leave
because that is what they always do
And no one has proved that wrong

No one will just sit with me
They all stay standing
Acting as if I am a damsel
In need of being saved

They dont know that I choose this
To stay in the world
Only seen by the dead
Because at least to them I can be helpful

The cold of the world
Will never touch me

Or maybe it has
And that is why I feel this way

Because like I said I am numb
Doesn't matter who you are
There will be no response
For I am dead

Fake Faces

Take the pain away
Don't touch me anymore
Close the door behind you
And never open it again

I put my head against the wall
The clock is ticking in my ear
Never to stop
Never to disappear

But that is the thing
I like to hear the sound
It lets me know
That I am still alive

And then I see the people
Start to fill my room
I look around
Seeing that they all wear masks

These fake faces all around me
Have never felt like home

I have always wanted to leave
But I couldn't

For I have a chain around my ankle
And more that attack my arms
That pin me here
To this place

That is why I couldn't leave
When you asked me too
But you would never understand
No one ever does

So I will stay here
In this room
Filled with people
That have fake faces
And slip my own mask
Into place.

Someone Else

You say you will always be there
Holding my hand
Not letting me fall
Not letting me walk on my own

But then you drop my hand
I begin to fall
And I am invisible to the world
Even to you

At the bottom of the pit
No one caught me
And I broke into
A thousand little pieces

For I thought you would never do that to me
It seems that now you are never there
I hold my breath
Pushing through the pain

As I put the pieces
Of myself back together

And though I trusted you
I now will never trust again

I am strong enough
To do this on my own
I am smart enough
Not to need anyone to save me again

I want to say thank you
For teaching me this important listen
To never put so much trust in one person
But I am a fighter to the core

I have picked myself up
And dusted myself off
Fixed the broken parts of me
And never again will I be a victim

You taught me to be one
A victim
Blaming others for what I feel
But being a Victim is easy

Now being a Surviver
That is hard
But that is what I am
I dont fear you

That is because
You dont deserve my fear

You are weak
For picking on those that are small

So since I now know
The lesson you had to teach
I think it is time
For you to go and teach
Someone else

Trust You

You tell me to close my eyes
And hold your hand
To trust with my whole heart
And to just jump

So I do what you say
Like the puppet that I am
But why should I
I listened to your lies

For way to long
I have been standing here
Looking down at the pit below
Just waiting for the courage

But I can't seem to find it
So, I sit right down
With legs over the edge
Just relaxing

The chains begin to come out
And they whined around my arms

Like snakes they climb them
Locking me into place

I jump off the cliff
To get away from the chains
But they don't keep me here
The chains begin to follow

I'm leaving this place behind
I'm sick of all these lies
And finally I know
You are no family of mine

World of Ruins

I want to scream
I want someone to care
But the land I live in
Is one of destruction and Chaos
The world of ruins
I walk around and watch
As people rot away
Held by the hands of a cruel God
Screaming in hunger and pain
Never to get their needs met

I walk through this world
Strangely satisfied by what I see
The people I held dear
Wither away
I was alive once
I held a flower in my hand
And then I began to die
Slowly and pleasantly
I turned dead
Never wanting to live

My heart turned cold
I looked to the darkness for comfort
I found it there
The pain and the fear
Vanished with the lies
My eyes turned cold as ice
As if explaining my torture
In this life
I have no hand to hold
No one to count on
But myself

No Superhero

Why can't you hear my thoughts
That's right
You aren't a mind reader
I wish you were
That would make everything easier

I want to see the future
To grip it in my hand
But it doesn't work that way
I'm no superhero
I'm just me

Wont you come away with me
Hold my hand as I drive
I want to be away from these chains
That for so long have bond me
I look back and see your smiling face
And for a moment I can't leave
But I move my legs
And my body follows suit
Walking away from this land

"Come with me" I say
"No I can't" You reply
"Why" I ask
No reply and you disappear
As if not meaning to be here
As if you never were

"Come fly" I call
You say "I don't believe"
And I fall
You always hurt me
By never believing in me

Why don't you believe
How can I be that much less
Then you
Why do your eyes
always look disappointed
When it comes to me
Why am I not good enough
For your love
That is all I want
But I guess that is to much
For you to give to me

But then again I am
No superhero
And I guess to you that
Makes me less
I know the feeling

I am a disappiontment
To myself
Why would anyone believe in me
When I don't believe in myself
That is asking to much
And so
I fade from existence.

The Movie

Take a seat
Watch me in the movie
Look at me dance and sing
Around the stage I go

Yet I sit in the audience
Watching me go
I hide my face in shame
For the things she says and does

But you sit laughing
Staring straight into my eyes
I see the look of love on your face
I'm still a little kid in my mind

Let me put on an act for you
Instead of saying what I truly feel
Mom and dad hold your heads up
Your kids a star

Watch me go as I turn
Around I go faster and faster

Not knowing what to say
You all would hate to see me fall

How could you?

Life was hard
And you made it harder
I should have known
By the way you smiled

You were family
He was just a guy
You mean more to me
But you threw it away

You helped me
I did a lot
We were good friends
But I guess that didn't mean much

We went through the same
And cried just as much
It affected us both
And when I needed someone you were there

Time flew by
We grew apart

Those wounds
Are now scars
Unhealed by time

The Clock

The clock with its ticking

The people with their nagging

And me with nothing

Not a peep

Not a whisper

Nothing happens

No feeling

No lies

No truth

No people to call

No one to talk too

No one will listen

No one will care

I guess I should say

That no one is my friend

And I am their's

Why can't anyone

Care for me

Maybe just

Once I want them too

Alone

Have you ever tried to scream
Over and over again
No matter how hard you try
Nothing will come out
Not even a peep

Then all of a sudden
You feel you don't belong
You can't see any walls
But they're there
Glass and Unbreakable

You want to scream
You try so hard
But still nothing comes out
That is when you know
You're alone

People throw loneliness around
Thinking it's a game
When those that are really alone
Can't be helped no matter

How hard they try

When you're alone you feel
Like a crack in a wall
That never gets fixed and
Ignored by the world

A Few Seconds

I walk down the dark hall
With the flicker of lights
Showing the true damage
Of the place I once called home
Closing my eyes I fall against these walls
Just remembering when life was fun
Before you hit the road

Bet you didn't know
Mama became depressed
I had to hide it from my sister
Mama turned to drugs and alcohol
But it was all the same in the end
Death came early for her
She is lucky too

You caught wind
Came back for a month or two
After that you left once again
And the house payment was do
I quit school so sister could go
We began to work things out

And all was fine

Until you came back
Stumbling half drunk
You slept and left in the middle of the night
My joyous face turns to tears
As I look at you dead
And I think if you would have stayed
You wouldn't and we wouldn't be this way

An Evil History

The words I utter
Fall heavy from these lips
Spoken of a time
Of great misery
I can not find comfort
In this place I used to call home
And it has become a scene of death
The happiness is drained from it
Never to return again
No one knows the story
Of the dreadful place and its past
The vision of those horrible scene
Runs over and over in my head
Some nights I wake up screaming
But nothing works
There is nothing I can do
No way to let this go
I can't forget anything
There is no way out
I've been running for way to long
I must go back
And face my fears

Tell Me How I Should Be

What should I say

When you make me mad

What should I say

When the time is not right

What should I do

When you say those things

What should I do

When time is to short

How do you want me to be

When things aren't going right

How do you want me to be

When I feel hurt inside

Tell me how I should act

And I might be that way

Begin to Fade

The footsteps begin to fade
With every step that falls
It echos on the walls
The shame that grows inside
The things that I hide
With ever step that falls

The days no longer cold
The nights go on forever
I am feeling all alone
The pace of the music quickens
The lights begin to shine
Blinding me from the path I need to go

My hands begin to ache
And I feel them beginning to go up
I'm told to smile
And I listen to the command
I fell my feet begin to move
I start to do a dance

I am a puppet

BEAUTIFULLY BROKEN

Doing what the puppet master wants
The lights begin to fade
I see the laughter that has come from me
And I want it all to stop
But it never will stop

Listen!

Why does it hurt so much
When no one listens
To me anymore
The crowd is leaving
And there I stand calling out
But they still leave
The room is white
The purest white
I begin to cry
And that leads
To my screaming
As I fall to my knees
You weren't there
And neither was anyone else
So I lay there
The clock ticking
Along with my heart
But they soon fade
Both in perfect unison
And I realized that no one ever cared
For if they did they would hear my cry
And they would have come to my aid

No one does though
Everyone left for reasons
Unknown to me
So there I lay
Counting your foot steps
I think it is at million
Not one of those
Came to me
See nobody cares

I'm Your Hero

Give me the questions
To these answers
Make me find my real self
Somewhere deep inside of me

Take my hand
And hold on tight
Do not close your eyes
Look down upon the world so free
And wonder why can't that be me

As you sleep so soundlessly
Remember that time does not stop
Try to reach the highest you can
Make sure you don't fall
At the bottom is what you most dread

Take my hand
And hold on tight
Do not close your eyes
Look down upon the world so free
And wonder why can't that be me

I will save you
From all your fears
Raise your head and hold it high
Wondering what's your alibi
I am your hero
Come to save the day

Take my hand
And hold on tight
Do not close your eyes
Look down upon the world so free
And wonder why can't that be me

Should I Cross the Road

I don't know if I should cross the road
The cars are coming
10 miles away
I could have gone
I should have gone
But I might have gotten hit
It's not worth it
Okay, I'm going to go
Oh, wait, another car is coming
I might get hit

Because of the Fighting

I used to be a person

In this world

But because of the fighting

And don't forget bickering

And add the violence and swearing

I have become one

Of the many

Zombie like people

Like I so hated

When I used to be different

Now I'm just one in the crowd

I remember the times

Were I actually felt

Now all I feel is numb

I hear myself swear

And talk about Violence

As if it were okay to do

And I fight with my parents

I think I'm not becoming the thing I hate

But in reality I am

I am one face in the crowd

The Real War

The soft beating of a drum
Over the gun shots
Of an unknown battle
Way far away
The men that had families
Lay dead around the ones from a foreign land
The red liquid starts to stain the ground
Most of them were friends
Comrades
Even brothers
Lay with Gus in their hands
By one another
We have almost won
But that is not a good price to pay

The Warm Sun

The warm sun puts its hands on me
And touches my cool skin
Making me warm inside
The fresh smell of the farms
Creeps into my nose
The sweet chirping of birds and laughter
Fills my ears with the same warmth
As the sun had
The warm breeze hits
My back and with one breath
Of its mighty lungs
Makes my papers go wild

The Special Wind

Sweeping over the grass
Making it shutter
As if it were a hawk
Looking for its prey
The wind is faster then a car
And seems to run a race
Beating the unknown person
Where the finish line is
Nobody knows
It carries a noise so
That sometimes it doesn't
Matter were you are
To hear it on the wind
Without the wind
Where would we get a breeze

I'm Sorry

I have not listened
To you the one I love
When you told me to clean

But I did get sidetracked
By the person on the phone
An I know you told me not to
But I still did

After the phone I realized
I was quite hungry
And couldn't clean on an empty stomach
So I made a sandwich
Making an even bigger mess

After that I decided to watch some T.V.
As I ate my sandwich
On the couch with no plate
Leaving the crumbs of my sandwich

When my T.V. program was over
I remember that I need to check

The thing that I'm addicted to
Tik Tok

By the time I got done with that
It was too late you were home
And that was why I didn't clean
So please forgive me
You the one I love

The Show

I begin to dance
The music starts off slow
And then it speeds up
It stops
I stop and introduce the next act
Out of breath
I walk calmly off the stage
I watch from the wing
The crowds favorite

She took my spot
She whirls and spins
The crowd begins to cheer
I see now
That this wasn't my show
I walk away
Into the darkness
But I smile
Cause my job is done

As I walk away
I hear the music stop

And the same guy
That held flowers off stage
For me
Now hold them for her

I am The Wind

I am the wind

Forever moving

Never staying in one place

Untamable to the world

I sweep about the place

I'm wild and free

On some days I'm calm

But other days I'm hyper

No one could ever catch me

I whip your hair from side to side

Never really thinking twice

My family doesn't understand

They aren't wild and free

But more so like big rocks

Making me stop

And coming in my way

But sometimes they don't even understand

They can't stop me

They use me to run away

And that's why people love me

But I never stay in one place long

Even though I leave

They follow me like they are clouds
They love me no matter what
I hate to leave them
So I stay a while
But then its time for me to go
And I hate to see them sad
The stories of where I have been
I only know
It doesn't matter to anyone
They love me all the same
When I try to tell them
They don't catch what I say
I have been a lot of places
But never stay for long
I have done that all my life
And I'm starting to hate it
I will go to many places
And in time I will come back
The world has left it for me to decide
I haven't chosen one place to stay
I know people will be leaving soon
Maybe I could follow them
Or maybe they will follow me
I have no place to call my home
I have always been this way
Even before my parents split
I remember being free
Blowing through the trees
Going where I want
Whenever I want

Testing the boundaries
Society could never train me
I will not jump through hoops
Just to be the same
I will not stop blowing
I take no commands
Because I'm wild and free
And I like to be that way
Nobody will be able to stop me
I am untamable and wild
I am the wind

No One Will Come

The light is shining down
In the cold little room
There is no bed and no furniture
The only thing in the room
Is me huddled in a corner
Away from the rest of the world

Closed in a room
Forgotten be all
With an unbreakable door
On it a lock
That has no key

Why am I so forgotten
When the world
Really needs me
But as forgotten I am

I have not heard one person
Who has dared to come
And find me
But surely you do remember

The time we had

Written on the Wall

I'm just sitting here
With my back against the wall
Waiting for someone to come
And find the writing on the wall

What it says is not good
I can't explain it
The writing on the wall
Is all I can say

Written in blood
Sealed with a kiss
It's almost a suicide note
And yet it's almost a love letter

Blood and wounds
Are only on the outside
But emotional damage is
On the inside

The person one faces
Lives in the back of our minds

And now that evil voice
Is moving to the front

So I'm sitting here
With my back to the wall
Waiting for someone to come
And find the writing on the wall

I Don't Belong

You see the world
It passes you by
You jump in
Only to realize
That you don't belong
Your an outsider
In a world ran by popularity
You want to get out
You try and try
You see the hallway getting longer
You almost reach it
The door knob in your grasp
You turn it
And find out it is locked
You pound on the door
Again and again
Finally it opens
And you wake up
And then
The world really passes you by
And darkness falls
In the world's foot steps

And then you turn
See something bright
And then
Everything goes dark

I am No Better

Why do I close my eyes
And look the other way
Do I pretend to be better
Then I really am
Then let me ask you this
Why do you close your eyes
And look the other way
When some poor kid needs you
Do you think you're better

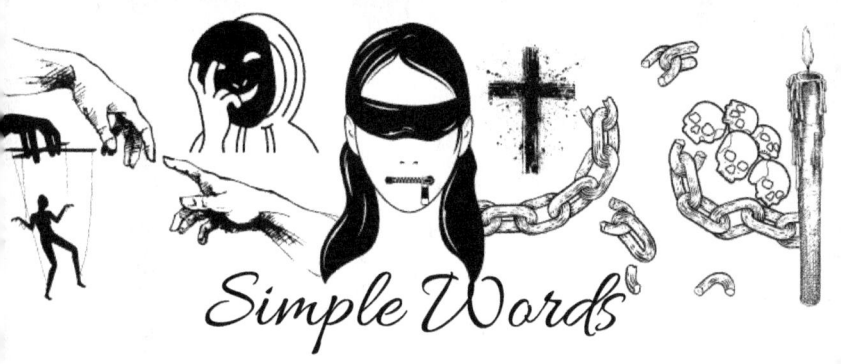

Simple Words

Darkness
Hides the pain

Love
The thing that kills us

Time
Goes to fast

Steps
Lead away from me

You
Never were there

Life
The loose soil under foot

Speed
To fast to care

A tree

Still as life should be

Dreaming
To good to wake from

Reality
To evil to be in

Nothing Just Nothing

I feel nothing

Not sadness

Or happiness

Neither madness

Nothing

I am not numb

Cause what I feel is worse

It's nothing

Pure nothing

Is what I feel

Just Go!

Why don't you go away
Like everyone else in my life
Walking out without a care
Never caring about anyone

People never really see
Whats down in my heart
The loneliness that consumes me
Leaving no joy

People only want to see
What is on the out
Never really seeing the inside
Not getting to know the truth

We don't choose how we look
And neither do our parents
But there is a reason why
We look and act different

People Always Leave

The world at your fingertips
And you just sit there
With a huge grin on your face
While the ones you love
Fall beneath the surface
Taken away from the pain
Regrat and scars
That were all put there by you

You hold the key to the way
And yet you don't open it
For you fear what that door holds
And your heart
Once loving and carefree
Is now as cold as the ice in my drink

But for me
I do not fall beneath
The surface and stay for one reason
And it is to remind you of the pain
Of the past and all the days to come
For when I fall beneath that surface

You will no longer remember who
You were at one time and
You will know the future that is to come

The Words of Life

Pain

Just a word

Or so I thought

But then I started

To feel it not caring

But I don't want to

Anymore I hate

It so much

Pain

Love

Not for friends

Really loving someone

Out there who knows you

Really well and really doesn't care

What you look like

Having them love

You back

Love

Tears

When you cry

Something happened
In you life that made
You sad and made you realize
You have these feelings in you
That you can never
Get rid of them
Sometimes it causes
Pain but don't
Worry it is fine
Tears

Freedom

The wind begins to blow
My hair lashes from side
To side like a whip in a cowboy's hand
The sound of voices and instruments
Fill my ears, thoughts of everything
Fills my head, as I ride down that road

Feeling free I have no boundaries
This is my escape from life
From everything that's gone wrong
To the best things
To the memories of old times
To what I'm living in right now
That's all taken when I
Go on a bike ride

The only thing there is to care about
Is the road, cars, not crashing
And the music that is being played
I can be as silly as I
Want and no one says anything
To me the speed of the bike

Makes me feel free
And it wipes away all the
Worry, Pain,
And memories

No One

I can't help but hide
The tears that I cry
I can't wipe away
This fake smile I have on

How come I have to hide
What I know inside
This pain keeps eating away
At the innocence that I hold

Can anyone really see
What is and truly me
With ever empty foot steps that I hear
Another tear begins to roll
Down this wet stained cheek

Sitting all alone in a room unlike my own
Feeling all alone in a world that's not my own
No one seems to listen
No one seems to care

They don't hear me yell

They don't even notice that I'm here
I walk down the halls
And I feel so invisible

No one is by my side
No one seems to care
No one can help me because
No one will listen

The Coming of Dark Times

I try to take away the pain
But whatever I try just ends up bring more
I can't stop these things I feel
And it seems that I can't really tell anyone
Not even myself

The secrets that are hidden
Of those evil times
Are locked in a box I can't destroy
I'm really getting tired of all the hurting
That I myself is causing

I hate seeing myself lie
I hate the smiles I'm forced to portray
I hate that my real self is somewhere forgotten
But what can I do to change

Everyone leans on me
And most of the time
I feel like I'm the one
With the world on my shoulders

I'm tired of pretending
Today is the day my real self
Is busting out
I keep trying to remember
Who that person is
But it seems so lost and dark times
Will be coming along with that person

The Place I Used to Call Home

The door is on one hinge
The roof has fallen in
I walk inside
To look at what happened
To the place I once called home

Some walls have fallen in
And the paint is coming off
The pictures now hang sideways
And some have fallen off
They are broken and cracked

I walk down the collapsing stairs
And look around the place
Remembering a lot of happy memories
And one by one they fade
Into the crumbling house

For this place has become
So much like the family I once had
Now the family and the house are destroyed

Never to return to true beauty again
And that makes me cry

I walk back up those stairs
That have now been laced by time
I reach down and pick up a photo
But it turns to ashes in my hand
I let it go in the wind

I hate what my life has become
A shell of a human who used to be
With this face that has stayed
And makes them believe I'm happy
But no matter this pain will never leave

At the Bus Stop

The beating of my heart
The pain that lies inside of this empty shell
The pain I cannot take anymore
I've tried to let it out

To watch my past is useless
And to watch the future is even more
All the times I spent with you
Will never be enough

I tried to listen, I've tried to calm down
I can't take this anymore
Because the blackness is getting to thick
And it's filling up my head

Why should I hold the pain
That wells up inside my head
Can I help the way I am
Even when I don't want to be that way at all

My true self lies dead
While the imposter takes over

I try to look away

I can not take this life anymore
I want to go away
The bus comes screeching to a hault
I am standing there waiting for the doors to open

But this bus does not come for me
It comes for what I use to be
And that is why it does not open it's door
And it will wait forever more

Locked Away

The world so blind inside
It's so cold and cruel
Only caring about ourselves
Living just to die
Never really knowing why
Just living to die

Locked away from the world
Out of fear for yourself
Never telling another
Never seeing another person
Can you really live like that
Locked away from all that you know
That really is no way to live

Even when people
Come to call for you
You turn them away
Not opening the door
Staying locked inside
Your castle
Safe inside your stone walls

One day someone will come
And tare down the walls
And bring you back
Into the world
And make you feel alive
Ready to live your life
Not live to die
Like you used to do

Escaping Reality

Oh, mind of mine take me away to the fictional land I want to play.
Where the pain I feel is like the white rabbit knowing he is
Running late and knowing the punishment but I will
No longer let it ruin my life. For if I stay, this pain
Will Eat away the little bit I have left. Leaving
me in a way I will be madder than the rest.

I want to be like Alice and slip down the rabbit hole.
Have a grand adventure and never pay the toll.
Being in a world of nonsense that makes
sense. Unlike the real world
That should make sense
But is utter nonsense.
Sounds nice to me.

Oh, mind,
Please mind!
Take me away!

I want to drink delicious hot tea with
The Hatter.

See the wild crazy grin of
The Cheshire Cat.

Feel the panic and pain of
The white rabbit
Being late.

But alas, I can not, I am as stuck as the binding
of new book pages. Forced to deal with the
pain inside. Never to be able to run
and hide. I must face it like the
Queen of Hearts screaming
"Off with their Heads"
Never can they see
me fail. They all
are watching

This little play that is my life.

www.ingramcontent.com/pod-product-compliance
Lightning Source LLC
LaVergne TN
LVHW022109220825
819394LV00034B/591